MW01109853

PRO FOOTBALL'S
MOST SPECTACULAR
QUARTERBACKS

by Michael Sandler

Consultant: Norries Wilson
Head Football Coach
Columbia University

BEARPORT
PUBLISHING

New York, New York

Credits
Cover and Title Page, center, © Chad Ryan/Cal Sport Media/Newscom; left, © AP Images/
NFL Photos; right, © AP Images/David Stluka; TOC-L, © AP Images/James D Smith;
TOC-R, © AP Images/David Stluka; 4, © AP Images/Paul Abell; 5L, © Allen Eyestone/The
Palm Beach Post/Zuma Press/Newscom; 5R, © Hunter Martin/NFL/Getty Images; 6, © AP
Images/NFL Photos; 7, © AP Images/James D Smith; 8, © NFL Photos/Getty Images; 9, ©
AP Images/Paul Spinelli; 10, © Chris McGrath/Getty Images; 11, © Preston Mack/Zuma
Press/Newscom; 12, © NFL Photos/Getty Images; 13, © AP Images/Sharon Ellman; 14,
© NFL Photos/Getty Images; 15, © Rob Tringali/Sportschrome/Getty Images; 16, © NFL
Photos/Getty Images; 17, © AP Images/NFL Photos; 18, © NFL Photos/Getty Images; 19,
© Tom Hauck/Getty Images; 20, © NFL Photos/Getty Images; 21, © Gary C. Caskey/UPI
Photo/Newscom; 22TL, © AP Images/James D Smith; 22TR, © AP Images/David Stluka;
22CL, © Scott Boehm/Getty Images; 22CR, © Jerome Davis/Icon SMI/Newscom; 22BL, ©
Rob Tringali/Sportschrome/Getty Images; 22BR, © Brian Snyder/Reuters/Landov.

Publisher: Kenn Goin
Senior Editor: Lisa Wiseman
Creative Director: Spencer Brinker
Design: Keith Plechaty
Photo Researcher: James O'Connor

Library of Congress Cataloging-in-Publication Data

Sandler, Michael, 1965–
  Pro football's most spectacular quarterbacks / by Michael Sandler.
      p. cm. — (Football-o-rama)
  Includes bibliographical references and index.
  ISBN-13: 978-1-936088-23-2 (library binding)
  ISBN-10: 1-936088-23-1 (library binding)
  1. Quarterbacks (Football) — United States— Biography. I. Title.
  GV939.A1S253 2011
  796.332092'2— dc22
  [B]
                            2010004284

For more information, write to Bearport Publishing Company, Inc., 45 West 21st St, Suite
3B, New York, New York 10010. Printed In the United States of America in North Mankato,
Minnesota.

072011
062311CGC

10 9 8 7 6 5 4 3

CONTENTS

MOST SPECTACULAR QUARTERBACKS

Professional quarterbacks are smart, brave, and athletic. They have to be. Their job—guiding an NFL team to victory—is one of the toughest and most complicated in all of sports.

Quarterbacks are the leaders of the **offensive team**. They are responsible for calling plays and making sure they're carried out. They have powerful arms that can accurately throw a ball. They can **scramble** and break free when a **sack** seems certain. The split-second decisions quarterbacks make while **defenders** are **rushing** in often mean the difference between a win and a loss.

New Orleans Saints quarterback Drew Brees looks to throw the ball during Super Bowl XLIV (44) in 2010.

4

The best quarterbacks need to be almost superhuman when the clock is ticking down and a touchdown is needed. Only the best can convince their teammates that there's still a chance to win and then go ahead and prove it.

In this book you'll meet the best of the best—Brett Favre, Drew Brees, Donovan McNabb, Tony Romo, Philip Rivers, Tom Brady, Aaron Rodgers, and Peyton Manning. It won't take long to see why they're considered the most spectacular quarterbacks in the NFL.

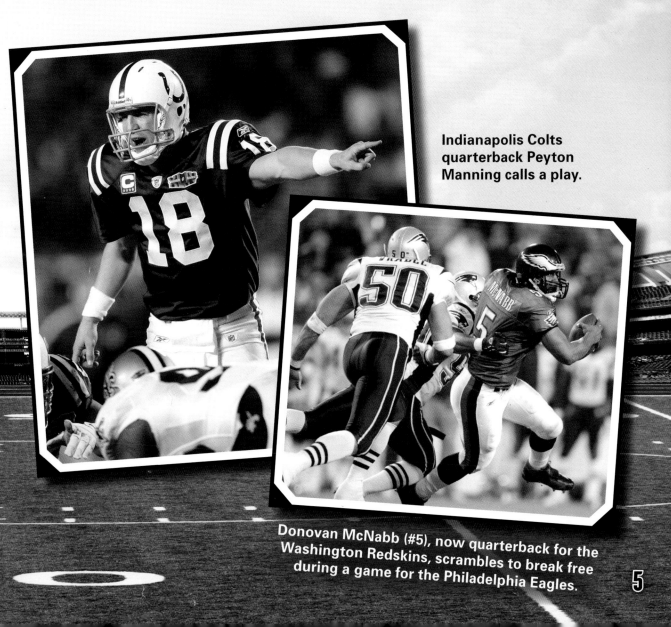

Indianapolis Colts quarterback Peyton Manning calls a play.

Donovan McNabb (#5), now quarterback for the Washington Redskins, scrambles to break free during a game for the Philadelphia Eagles.

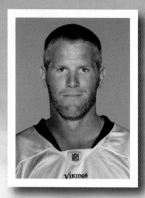

BRETT FAVRE #4
MINNESOTA VIKINGS

Born: 10/10/1969 in Gulfport, Mississippi
Height: 6′ 2″ (1.88 m)

Weight: 222 pounds (101 kg)
College: Southern Mississippi
Pro Bowls: 11

Nobody wins like Brett Favre. From 1991 through 2009, he racked up an NFL record of 181 victories—50 more than any other **active** quarterback! Most of these wins came in the 16 seasons that he spent with the Green Bay Packers.

Brett retired from the NFL in 2008, but then quickly changed his mind. He loved football too much to quit. He returned to the game first with the New York Jets in 2008 and then with the Minnesota Vikings in 2009.

Incredibly, Brett's right arm still showed the same zip that it had when he'd entered the league nearly 20 years earlier. Behind its power, the Vikings made it into the 2009–2010 playoffs and a meeting with the Dallas Cowboys. How did the game with Dallas turn out? A win for Brett and Minnesota, naturally!

HIGHLIGHTS

1995–1996	Earned his first NFL Most Valuable Player Award (MVP)
1996–1997	Led Green Bay to a 35-21 win over New England in Super Bowl XXXI (31); earned his second NFL MVP Award
2009–2010	Led the Vikings to a playoff win and a trip to the **NFC Championship Game**; threw for more than 4,000 yards (3,658 m) for the sixth time in his career

Brett threw four touchdowns in the 34-3 win against Dallas in the 2009–2010 playoffs. He also became the oldest starting quarterback in NFL playoff history!

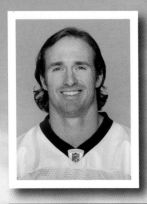

DREW BREES #9
NEW ORLEANS SAINTS

Born: 1/15/1979 in Austin, Texas
Height: 6' 0" (1.83 m)
Weight: 209 pounds (95 kg)

College: Purdue
Pro Bowls: 4

"You're too short." Drew Brees has heard people say this hundreds of times. Most NFL coaches, general managers, and **scouts** think quarterbacks need to be tall to succeed. Barely 6' 0" (1.83 m) tall, Drew gets up on his toes while throwing to make up for his lack of height. "I don't know what it's like to be 6' 5" (1.96 m)," he says. "I don't know what those guys see."

Somehow Drew sees well enough to find open **receivers** and throw crisp, accurate passes. Add in his ability to **inspire** his teammates and he's one of the league's top quarterbacks. Says teammate Carl Nicks, "If he told me to jump off a cliff in order to win a game, I'd do it."

While Carl and his teammates haven't gone to such extremes, they certainly do know how to win. On February 7, 2010, Drew led the Saints all the way to victory in Super Bowl XLIV (44).

HIGHLIGHTS

2006–2007	Led New Orleans to the team's first NFC title game
2008–2009	Became the only passer in NFL history besides Dan Marino to throw for over 5,000 yards (4,572 m) in a season
2009–2010	Named MVP of Super Bowl XLIV (44); led the NFL in **quarterback rating, completion percentage**, and touchdown passes

Drew completed 32 of 39 passes in the Saints' 31-17 win over the Indianapolis Colts in Super Bowl XLIV (44).

DONOVAN McNABB #5
WASHINGTON REDSKINS

Born: 11/25/1976 in Chicago, Illinois
Height: 6' 2" (1.88 m)
Weight: 240 pounds (109 kg)

College: Syracuse
Pro Bowls: 6

In 11 seasons with the Philadelphia Eagles, Donovan McNabb didn't always have a lot of help. The Eagles rarely had great receivers or **running backs** to play next to him.

Luckily, Donovan overcame his team's lack of stars. His scrambling skills let him leave the **pocket** to run the ball himself. His ability to throw the ball quickly let him release passes before the rush arrived. These talents helped Donovan lead the Eagles into one Super Bowl, five NFC Championship Games, and eight playoff appearances.

In April 2010, Donovan was traded to the Washington Redskins. If Washington surrounds him with the support he lacked in Philadelphia, he may finally achieve his dream—a Super Bowl win!

HIGHLIGHTS

2004–2005	Led Philadelphia to its first Super Bowl appearance in more than 20 years
2008–2009	Led Philadelphia into the NFC Championship Game for the fifth time
2009–2010	Led Philadelphia into the playoffs for the eighth time in his career

Donovan looks to pass the ball for Philadelphia during Super Bowl XXXIX (39).

TONY ROMO #9
DALLAS COWBOYS

Born: 4/21/1980 in San Diego, California
Height: 6′ 2″ (1.88 m)

Weight: 226 pounds (103 kg)
College: Eastern Illinois
Pro Bowls: 3

In Dallas, a quarterback's greatness is measured by his playoff wins. Famous Cowboys passers such as Troy Aikman and Roger Staubach had plenty of them. Tony Romo, unfortunately, lost his first two playoff games. Some people blamed Tony. That's why, despite breaking almost every team passing record in 2009, Tony still had critics.

In January 2010, Tony proved his critics wrong. He outplayed Donovan McNabb in a playoff win against the Philadelphia Eagles. Tony didn't throw one **interception** as he picked apart Philadelphia's defense with one sharp pass after another. His two touchdowns were key to Dallas's 34-14 win. Most Cowboy fans believe there will be many more victories to come.

HIGHLIGHTS

2006-2007	Took over as the starting quarterback for Dallas; led the Cowboys into the playoffs
2007-2008	Led Dallas to an **NFC East** title; set a Dallas team record with 36 passing touchdowns
2009-2010	Helped Dallas to its first playoff win in 13 years

On January 9, 2010, Tony got his first playoff win during a game against the Philadelphia Eagles.

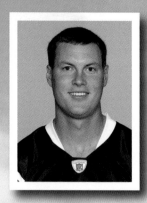

PHILIP RIVERS #17
SAN DIEGO CHARGERS

Born: 12/8/1981 in Decatur, Alabama
Height: 6' 5" (1.96 m)
Weight: 228 pounds (103 kg)

College: North Carolina State
Pro Bowls: 2

In fifth grade, Philip Rivers made a few wishes. He wanted a baby brother and an NFL career. Luckily, both wishes came true. He got his brother first. Then, a decade later, in 2004, he joined the San Diego Chargers.

At first, Philip was Drew Brees's **backup**. Then San Diego let Drew go, gambling that Philip could do the job. He proved the team right. In 2006, he powered San Diego to a 14-2 record, the best in team history. The following year, he led the Chargers to their first playoff win since 1994. With a **quick release** and talent for last-minute comebacks, Philip is probably the NFL's best young quarterback.

HIGHLIGHTS

2006-2007	Guided San Diego to a 14-2 record and the **AFC West** title
2008-2009	Led the NFL in both quarterback rating and passing touchdowns (34)
2009-2010	Helped San Diego into the playoffs for the fourth straight season

Philip passes the ball during the January 2010 AFC playoff game against the New York Jets.

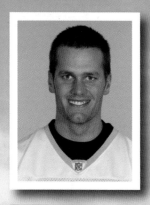

TOM BRADY #12
NEW ENGLAND PATRIOTS

Born: 8/3/1977 in San Mateo, California
Height: 6′ 4″ (1.93 m)
Weight: 225 pounds (102 kg)

College: Michigan
Pro Bowls: 5

One thing sets Tom Brady apart from every other active NFL quarterback—he's won three Super Bowl titles! Title number one came in Tom's very first season as a Patriot starter in 2001–2002. The former backup player brought New England into Super Bowl XXXVI (36) against the mighty St. Louis Rams. The game turned Tom into a New England **legend**. He marched his team downfield to set up the winning field goal just as time ran out.

Since then, Tom's legend has grown even bigger with two more Super Bowl titles. Except for two seasons when he was hurt, the Patriots haven't missed the playoffs with Tom as quarterback.

HIGHLIGHTS

2001–2002	Named MVP of Super Bowl XXXVI (36); at the time, 24-year-old Tom was the youngest quarterback in history to win a Super Bowl
2003–2004	Led the Patriots to victory in Super Bowl XXXVIII (38); was named Super Bowl MVP
2004–2005	Earned his third league title in Super Bowl XXXIX (39)
2007–2008	Led the league in quarterback rating, completion percentage, and passing yards; named NFL MVP

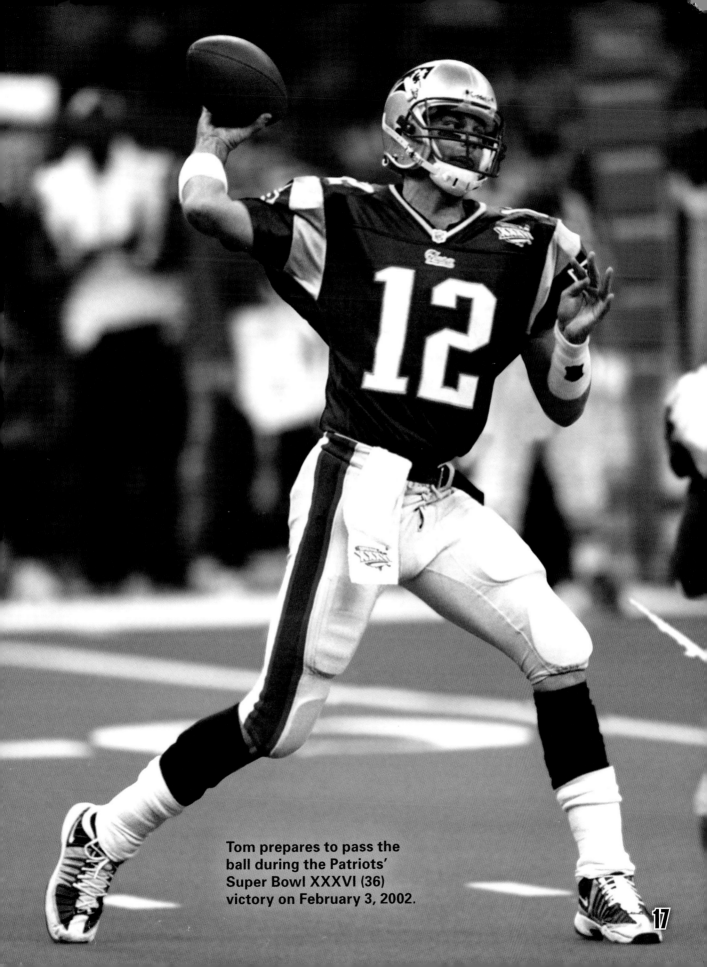

Tom prepares to pass the ball during the Patriots' Super Bowl XXXVI (36) victory on February 3, 2002.

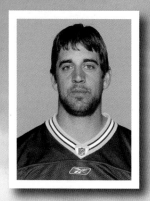

AARON RODGERS #12
GREEN BAY PACKERS

Born: 12/2/1983 in Chico, California
Height: 6' 2" (1.88 m)
Weight: 220 pounds (100 kg)

College: California
Pro Bowls: 1

Replacing a legend isn't easy. When Aaron Rodgers became the Green Bay Packers' quarterback in 2008, he took a spot Brett Favre had held for 16 seasons. Many fans weren't sure he was up to the task.

Aaron quickly impressed the doubters, however, with both his strong arm and his toughness. Making the playoffs in his second season also helped. Packer fans will never forget Brett Favre, but they're learning to love Aaron.

"I've kind of made my career by proving some people wrong," he said. "It's going to be with me my entire career in the NFL, and I'm fine with that."

HIGHLIGHTS

2008–2009	Joined Kurt Warner as the only other first-year starting quarterback in history to throw for more than 4,000 yards (3,658 m)
2009–2010	Led Green Bay into the playoffs; was voted into the Pro Bowl for the first time

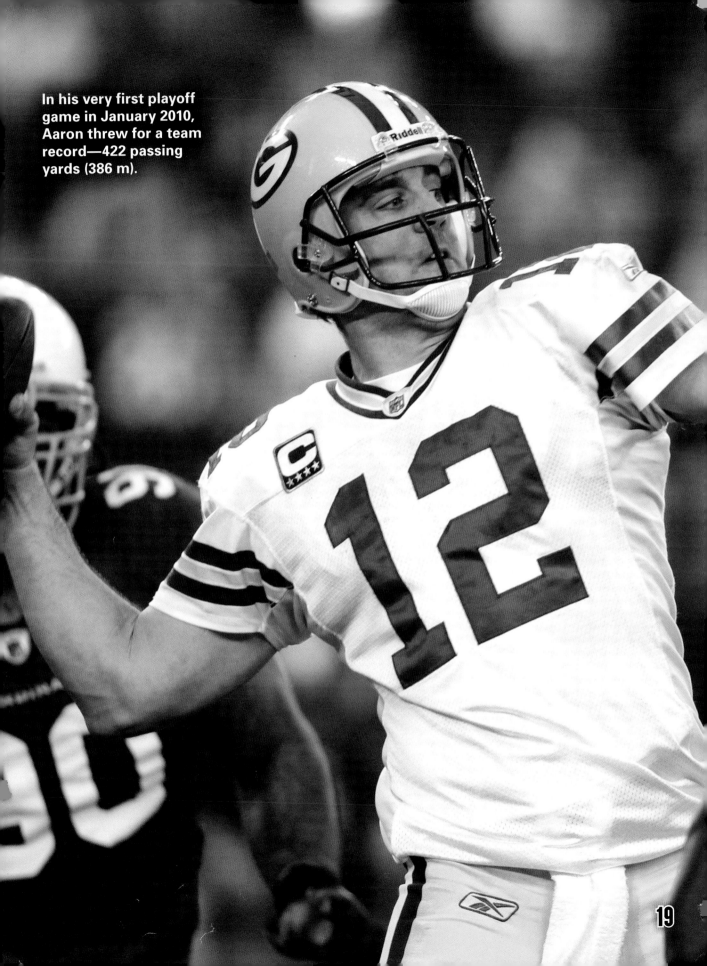

In his very first playoff game in January 2010, Aaron threw for a team record—422 passing yards (386 m).

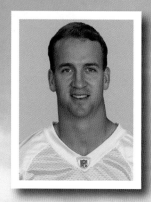

PEYTON MANNING #18
INDIANAPOLIS COLTS

Born: 3/24/1976 in New Orleans, Louisiana
Height: 6' 5" (1.96 m)

Weight: 230 pounds (104 kg)
College: Tennessee
Pro Bowl Selections: 10

Among the NFL's great quarterbacks, one stands especially tall. Peyton Manning boasts the perfect arm, great timing, and an incredible understanding of the game.

His coaches always trust him to make the right decision. Most passers just carry out plays that coaches choose—not Peyton. He decides many of the plays himself, right there at the **line of scrimmage**.

Of course, playing well in a big game is a great quarterback's biggest test. Peyton passed his test in Super Bowl XLI (41). He took MVP honors as the Colts overwhelmed the Chicago Bears with a 29-17 win. When it comes to quarterbacks, none are more spectacular than Peyton.

HIGHLIGHTS

2003–2004	Named NFL MVP
2004–2005	Named NFL MVP
2006–2007	Led the Colts to victory over the Chicago Bears in Super Bowl XLI (41); was named Super Bowl MVP
2008–2009	Named NFL MVP
2009–2010	Named NFL MVP; led the Colts into Super Bowl XLIV (44)

Peyton passes the ball during Super Bowl XLI (41).

MOST SPECTACULAR ALL-TIME RECORDS

Most Wins as Starting Quarterback (entire career)

Brett Favre.............181
John Elway 148
Dan Marino 147
Peyton Manning........131

Brett Favre

Most Passing Touchdowns (single season)

Tom Brady 50
(2007)

Peyton Manning 49
(2004)

Dan Marino 48
(1984)

Dan Marino 44
(1986)

Tom Brady

Most Passing Touchdowns (entire career)

Brett Favre............ 497
Dan Marino 420
Peyton Manning....... 366
Fran Tarkenton 342

Peyton Manning

Most Passing Yards (single season)

Dan Marino .....5,084 yards
(1984)   (4,649 m)

Drew Brees .....5,069 yards
(2008)   (4,635 m)

Kurt Warner.....4,830 yards
(2001)   (4,417 m)

Tom Brady ......4,806 yards
(2007)   (4,395 m)

Drew Brees

GLOSSARY

active (AK-tiv) when an athlete is still playing; not retired

AFC West (AY-EFF-SEE WEST) one of the four divisions in the NFL's American Football Conference (AFC)

backup (BAK-uhp) a player who doesn't play at the start of a game

completion percentage (kuhm-PLEE-shuhn pur-SEN-tij) a statistic that measures the percentage of a quarterback's passes that are caught by his receivers

defenders (di-FEND-urz) players who have the job of stopping the other team from scoring

inspire (in-SPIRE) to encourage; to motivate

interception (*in*-tur-SEP-shuhn) a pass caught by a defensive player on the other team, rather than the offensive player on the team that it was intended for

legend (LEJ-uhnd) a person who becomes very famous for a talent or an action

line of scrimmage (LINE UHV SKRIM-ij) an imaginary line across the field where the ball is put at the beginning of a play

NFC Championship Game (EN-EFF-SEE CHAM-pee-uhn-ship GAME) a playoff game that decides which National Football Conference (NFC) team will go to the Super Bowl

NFC East (EN-EFF-SEE EEST) one of the four divisions in the NFL's National Football Conference (NFC)

offensive team (aw-FEN-siv TEEM) the players who are responsible for scoring points

pocket (POK-it) a protected area on the field created by players so that the quarterback can drop back to throw the ball

quarterback rating (KWOR-tur-bak RAYT-ing) a measuring tool used by the NFL to compare the overall passing performance of league quarterbacks

quick release (KWIK ri-LEESS) the ability to throw the ball very quickly

receivers (ri-SEE-vurz) players whose job it is to catch passes

running backs (RUHN-ing BAKS) players who carry the ball on running plays

rushing (RUHSH-ing) trying to tackle a quarterback or interfering with his ability to carry out a play

sack (SAK) to tackle a quarterback behind the line of scrimmage while he's attempting to throw a pass

scouts (SKOUTS) people who search for talented players to play on professional teams

scramble (SKRAM-buhl) to run away from defenders to avoid being tackled

BIBLIOGRAPHY

The New York Times

The Sporting News

Sports Illustrated

NFL.com

pro-football-reference.com

READ MORE

Sandler, Michael. *Brett Favre (Football Heroes Making a Difference)*. New York: Bearport (2009).

Sandler, Michael. *Drew Brees and the New Orleans Saints: Super Bowl XLIV (Super Bowl Superstars)*. New York: Bearport (2011).

Sandler, Michael. *Peyton Manning and the Indianapolis Colts: Super Bowl XLI (Super Bowl Superstars)*. New York: Bearport (2008).

Sandler, Michael. *Tom Brady and the New England Patriots: Super Bowl XXXVIII (Super Bowl Superstars)*. New York: Bearport (2008).

LEARN MORE ONLINE

To learn more about the NFL's most spectacular quarterbacks, visit
www.bearportpublishing.com/FootballORama

INDEX